American Moments

ABDO
& Daughters

THE ASSASSINATION OF
MARTIN LUTHER KING JR.

By Alan Pierce

Published by ABDO Publishing Company, 4940 Viking Drive, Suite 622, Edina, Minnesota 55435. Copyright © 2005 by Abdo Consulting Group, Inc. International copyrights reserved in all countries. No part of this book may be reproduced in any form without written permission from the publisher. ABDO & Daughters™ is a trademark and logo of ABDO Publishing Company.

Printed in the United States.

Edited by: Melanie A. Howard
Interior Production and Design: Terry Dunham Incorporated
Cover Design: Mighty Media
Photos: AP/Wide World, Corbis, Library of Congress

Library of Congress Cataloging-in-Publication Data

Pierce, Alan, 1966-
    The assassination of Martin Luther King, Jr. / Alan Pierce.
        p. cm. -- (American moments)
    Includes index.
    ISBN 1-59197-727-4
    1. King, Martin Luther, Jr., 1929-1968--Assassination--Juvenile literature. I. Title. II. Series.

E185.97.K5P473 2005
323'.092--dc22
[B]
                                                    2004046443

CONTENTS

A NATION'S LOSS

The Reverend Dr. Martin Luther King Jr. had championed the rights of African Americans for many years. His efforts had won him admiration throughout the world. But King was also one of the most hated men in the United States. He frequently received death threats. Many people despised King's mission to advance racial equality.

A dispute brought King to Memphis, Tennessee. The workers who hauled the city's garbage wanted better wages and improved working conditions. They also wanted to form a union to negotiate a new contract with the city. The city refused to recognize the union. On February 12, 1968, most of the city's 1,300 African-American sanitation workers went on strike. King had arrived to organize marches in support of the workers.

On April 4, King was staying at the Lorraine Motel in Memphis. He shared a room with his friend and associate the Reverend Ralph Abernathy. King and his aides had received an invitation to attend dinner at the home of the Reverend Samuel Kyles. Kyles arrived at the motel while King and his aides prepared to go to dinner.

King walked out to the motel balcony and leaned on the railing. He chatted with some aides who had gathered in the courtyard below him. His driver, Solomon Jones, suggested that King wear a coat because the evening was becoming chilly.

Martin Luther King Jr.

LORRAINE MOTEL

Because of poor business, the Lorraine Motel property foreclosed in 1982. The Martin Luther King Jr. Memorial Foundation raised $144,000 to save the property. In 1987, the Lorraine Civil Rights Foundation began work on creating a museum at the Lorraine Motel. The National Civil Rights Museum (NCRM) opened on September 28, 1991. Its exhibits show the history of civil rights movements from the 1600s to the present.

Sign outside the Lorraine Motel

At 6:01 PM, a bullet struck King. In the courtyard, aides dropped to the ground and took cover behind a car. Abernathy came to King's side and tried to comfort the stricken leader. Soon, an ambulance arrived and rushed King to St. Joseph's Hospital. Doctors worked to save King, but the injury was fatal. King was pronounced dead at 7:05 PM.

King's death jolted the nation. But the assassination provoked different reactions among people. Many African Americans were enraged, and riots broke out in more than 100 cities. Some white Americans rejoiced that King was dead. On the national level, King's death was seen as the loss of an important American. President Lyndon B. Johnson declared a day of national mourning. The president also ordered U.S. flags to fly at half-mast in honor of King.

For some people, King was a hero who fought for justice.

From left: *Hosea Williams, Jesse Jackson, King, and Ralph Abernathy stand on the balcony of the Lorraine Motel.*

King's work gave hope to many African Americans. However, many whites felt threatened by King's actions. King prompted these feelings because he challenged racism. And there were those who did not want to see King's dream of racial equality realized.

SEPARATE BUT NOT EQUAL

With this dream, King dedicated himself to fighting a problem with a long history. For about 300 years, whites and blacks had lived in an unequal relationship in the United States. This situation had its origins in slavery. In the seventeenth century, England established colonies along the eastern coast of the continent. England also imported slaves from Africa to work on plantations in many southern colonies such as Virginia and Maryland. By about 1660, slavery became legally defined in some colonies. Slaves were considered property and served their masters for life.

Slavery continued even after the colonies gained their independence from English rule in the Revolutionary War. Although most Northern states had outlawed slavery by the early nineteenth century, slavery continued to thrive in the South. This was because the South's economy was based on agriculture, and slaves were used to plant and harvest crops. Northern states depended on employees who earned wages to work in factories.

Abraham Lincoln

The conflict over slavery contributed to the outbreak of the Civil War. In 1860, Abraham Lincoln was elected president. Lincoln did not

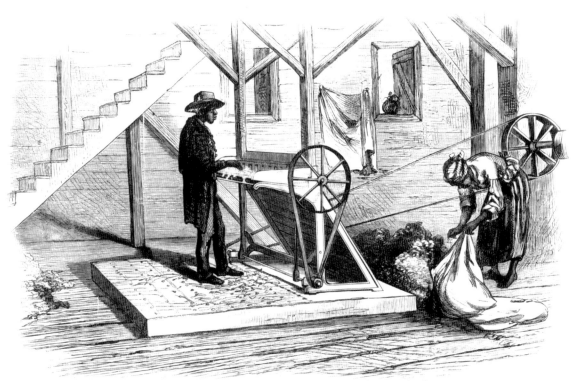

Slaves operate a cotton gin, which removes seeds from cotton.

want to abolish slavery, but he did wish to prevent it from spreading in the country. In response to Lincoln's election, 11 Southern states broke away from the United States between 1860 and 1861.

War erupted between the Northern and Southern states. The Northern states were known as the Union, while the Southern states made up the Confederacy. After four years of fighting, the Union army had defeated the Confederate forces. The Union victory had two important results. It preserved the unity of the United States. And it also led to the end of slavery.

At the end of the Civil War, four million freed slaves lived in the South. In the period known as Reconstruction, the United States faced the problem of how to help the former slaves. One of the nation's first acts was to abolish slavery. In 1865, most state legislatures passed the Thirteenth Amendment to the Constitution. This amendment prohibited slavery in the United States.

Congress and state legislatures ratified other constitutional amendments intended to protect African Americans. The Fourteenth Amendment was ratified in July 1868. It guaranteed state and U.S. citizenship to African Americans. The Fifteenth Amendment was included in the Constitution in 1870. This amendment was designed to strengthen voting rights for African-American men.

Despite these constitutional amendments, African Americans continued to experience the cruelties of racism in the South. Violent groups such as the Ku Klux Klan attacked African Americans and those who supported African-American rights. The Klan especially wanted to keep African Americans from voting. In order to create fear, Klan members whipped and murdered African Americans.

Southerners found other ways to deny African Americans the right to vote. Some Southern states used literacy tests. These tests required people to demonstrate their literacy before they were allowed to vote. Often, people were asked to interpret difficult material such as the state constitution. An official then determined whether the person was qualified to vote.

Another method used to keep African Americans from voting was the poll tax. People were compelled to pay this tax when they registered to vote. However, many African Americans had low-paying jobs and lacked the money to pay this tax. Both the poll tax and the literacy test reduced the number of registered African-American voters in the South.

African Americans also faced segregation in the South. Segregation was the system used to separate whites and blacks. This practice was sometimes referred to as Jim Crow. The term *Jim Crow* came from a song performed by a white minstrel named Thomas Dartmouth

A member of the Ku Klux Klan discourages African Americans from voting.

"Daddy" Rice in 1828. No one is certain why segregation came to be identified with Jim Crow. But Jim Crow was first used to describe segregation on trains in Massachusetts in the 1840s.

In the South, segregation grew more widespread in the 1890s. States passed laws that separated blacks and whites in schools, parks, hospitals, and the workplace. African Americans and whites also used different building entrances and drank from different water fountains. Signs reading "Whites Only" and "Colored Only" marked separate facilities. Segregation became so complete that black and white witnesses swore on different Bibles in the courtroom.

Segregation also existed on public transportation. In Louisiana, a state law required railroads to operate separate passenger cars for blacks and whites. A group of African Americans in the state decided to challenge the law. In June 1892, a man of African-American ancestry named Homer Plessy boarded a car reserved for whites. Plessy was arrested and appeared in court before Judge John H. Ferguson. Plessy was convicted and filed a lawsuit against Ferguson.

The U.S. Supreme Court heard the case of *Plessy v. Ferguson* in 1896. The Court ruled against Plessy and supported Louisiana's segregation law. Moreover, the court asserted that segregated facilities were legal as long as they were equal. This ruling established the "separate but equal" precedent. However, facilities for African Americans were almost always unequal.

By the early twentieth century, most African Americans suffered a hard existence in the South. They lost political power because whites denied them the right to vote. Segregation forced African Americans to go to inferior schools and other lesser facilities. This is the society that Martin Luther King Jr. knew as a child and young man.

A young girl reads in a segregated school in March 1942.

FROM STUDENT TO REVEREND

Martin Luther King Jr.'s family played an important role in the Baptist church in Atlanta, Georgia. King's grandfather, A. D. Williams, served as pastor of Ebenezer Baptist Church. Ebenezer was one of the most prominent African-American Baptist churches in Atlanta. In 1926, Williams's daughter, Alberta, married Martin Luther King Sr. Soon, King Sr. became an assistant pastor at Ebenezer.

The Kings had a daughter, Christine, in 1927. Their first son, Martin Luther King Jr., was born January 15, 1929, in Atlanta. Another son, Alfred Daniel, was born in 1930. The family lived in a thriving African-American business district.

In 1931, A. D. Williams died and Martin Luther King Sr. became pastor of Ebenezer. King Sr. worked to make Ebenezer even better. He improved the church with building projects. Membership grew from several hundred to several thousand.

Martin Luther King Sr. was a successful pastor. But this did not prevent his son, Martin, from feeling the shame of racism. As a child, Martin Luther King Jr. was friends with a white boy, whose father owned a business near the King home. When they were about 6 years old, the two boys attended different schools. King went to a segregated school for African Americans. Soon, King lost his white friend because the child's father no longer wanted the two boys to play together.

Ebenezer Baptist Church

When he was older, King finished his high school education early. He skipped grades 9 and 12. This advancement allowed him to enroll at Morehouse College in Atlanta at age 15. While at Morehouse, King decided to enter the ministry. Before he received his degree, King became an ordained minister. In 1948, he earned a bachelor's degree in sociology from the college.

Next, King entered Crozer Theological Seminary in Chester, Pennsylvania. Crozer was an outstanding school. And King also wanted to study in the North where segregation did not legally exist.

THE MAHATMA

Mohandas Karamchand Gandhi

Mohandas Karamchand Gandhi was born on October 2, 1869, in Porbandar, India. His Hindu religion taught him from an early age to believe that it was wrong to harm any living thing. Gandhi later used this principle to build his philosophy of nonviolent political protest.

In the 1890s, Gandhi began his career as a political protester in South Africa, which was a British colony. Under British rule, Indians suffered injustice and prejudice in South Africa. Gandhi worked for Indians' rights, which made him a well-known political figure.

Later, Gandhi introduced the satyagraha technique of political protest. Satyagraha, or "devotion to truth," encouraged resistance through inviting violence on oneself instead of inflicting it on others.

Gandhi returned to India in 1915. India, like South Africa, was a British colony. Gandhi led protests in support of greater rights for Indians. Eventually, he worked for India's independence from British rule. India achieved independence in 1947.

People began calling him the Mahatma, or "the great soul." In January 1948, Gandhi was shot and killed by Nathuram Godse, a Hindu fanatic.

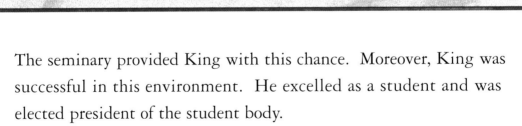

The seminary provided King with this chance. Moreover, King was successful in this environment. He excelled as a student and was elected president of the student body.

At Crozer, King learned about the teachings and practices of Mohandas Gandhi. King heard about Gandhi in a lecture given by

Mordecai Johnson. Johnson, who was the president of Howard University in Washington DC, had recently been in India. He believed that Gandhi's nonviolent methods could be used to help the racial troubles in the United States. King was impressed with what he heard about Gandhi.

In 1951, King received a bachelor of divinity degree from Crozer. He had graduated at the top of his class. His superb grades allowed him to continue his education. King chose to study theology at Boston University in Boston, Massachusetts.

While in Boston, King met a woman named Coretta Scott. She was from Alabama, but was studying music at the New England Conservatory of Music in Boston. The two were married in Alabama in June 1953.

The following year, King agreed to serve as pastor at the Dexter Avenue Baptist Church in Montgomery, Alabama. Accepting the position meant that he was returning to the segregated South.

At this time, segregation was coming under attack. In Topeka, Kansas, Oliver Brown's daughter, Linda, was not allowed to attend a white school near their home. Brown and other African-American families filed a lawsuit against Topeka's board of education. The suit claimed that segregation violated the Fourteenth Amendment.

Eventually, the case *Brown v. Board of Education of Topeka* went to the U.S. Supreme Court. On May 17, 1954, the Court issued a decision. The Court ruled that racial segregation in public schools violated the Fourteenth Amendment. Moreover, the Court overturned the "separate but equal" precedent of the *Plessy v. Ferguson* decision. Separate but equal facilities were inherently unequal, the Court decided.

MONTGOMERY

As controversy swirled in the South, King remained busy at Dexter Avenue Baptist Church. He preached at the church and presided over weddings and funerals. In 1955, he received his doctorate degree from Boston University. On November 17, the Kings' first child, Yolanda, was born.

Less than two weeks later, segregation came under attack in Montgomery. This challenge came against the city's segregated bus system. In Montgomery, the first ten bus seats were reserved for white passengers. African-American passengers sat in the rear ten seats. Riders in the middle seats were also divided by race. But black and white passengers were not allowed to sit in the same row. The arrangement meant black passengers sometimes had to give up their seats to whites.

On December 1, 1955, an African-American woman named Rosa Parks was riding a bus home. The driver asked her to give up her seat to a white man. She refused and was arrested. An African American had never before been charged with breaking the city's segregation laws.

African-American women in Montgomery called for a boycott of the city's buses. On December 2, Montgomery pastors and city leaders met at Dexter Avenue Baptist Church to discuss the boycott.

SHE WOULD NOT BE MOVED

Rosa Parks

Rosa Louise McCauley Parks was born on February 4, 1913 in Tuskegee, Alabama. By 1955, she was a seamstress and active in the National Association for the Advancement of Colored People (NAACP). Parks served as the secretary of the NAACP chapter in Montgomery, Alabama.

Because of her role in the Montgomery Bus Boycott, Parks has been called the "mother of the Civil Rights Movement." The boycott launched Martin Luther King Jr. as a public figure. In 1999, Parks was given the Congressional Gold Medal of Honor. This is the highest award that a civilian can earn in the United States.

They distributed leaflets about the boycott and told people about it in church. King was one of those who made copies of leaflets.

On December 5, King and other leaders met again. They formed the Montgomery Improvement Association (MIA) to manage the boycott. The Reverend Ralph Abernathy suggested the name for the group. He was a pastor, and also King's friend.

The ministers elected King as president of the MIA. He was only 26 years old at the time. But the ministers supported King because he had not made enemies in Montgomery. Also, he had shown admirable leadership as pastor of his church.

One of the MIA's tasks was to organize car pools for the boycotters. The transportation committee was responsible for this undertaking. The committee gathered cars and more than 200 volunteer drivers. It also set up a command post to take calls from people who needed rides. Yet, some African Americans continued to walk.

King discourages mob violence after his house is bombed.

African Americans expected the city to grant their demands. They did not seek to end segregation on buses. However, they wanted a seating system in which African Americans would not have to give up their seats. In addition, they wanted African-American drivers to drive routes used mainly by black passengers. MIA members met with city leaders and representatives from the bus company to resolve the dispute. But little progress was made.

As the boycott continued, King became a target. He received several threatening letters each day. On the night of January 30, 1956, a stick of dynamite exploded on King's porch. He was not home, but Coretta and Yolanda were. They were not hurt in the attack, which damaged the porch and shattered glass in the home. African Americans angry about the bombing gathered at King's home. King, however, urged them to be calm.

By this time, King was becoming a stronger believer in nonviolent protest. A large reason for this change was the influence of Bayard Rustin. He was an African-American activist who had supported India's independence from Britain. Rustin had also studied Gandhi's beliefs about nonviolence. He arrived in Montgomery and became one of King's advisers.

Meanwhile, the MIA filed a lawsuit in federal court that contested segregation on Alabama buses. The MIA filed the lawsuit on behalf of Aurelia S. Browder and other African Americans. The MIA's lawsuit was aimed at Montgomery mayor W.A. Gayle and other city officials. This case became known as *Browder v. Gayle.*

On June 5, 1956, federal judges ruled that segregation on Alabama's buses was unconstitutional. The ruling, however, did not end the boycott. The city of Montgomery appealed the decision to the U.S. Supreme Court.

On November 13, 1956, the U.S. Supreme Court also ruled that bus segregation was unconstitutional. The city wanted the case heard again, but by December, the legal fight was over. Montgomery's buses became desegregated. On December 21, 1956, King rode near the front of a Montgomery bus. The boycott had lasted more than 380 days. But it had helped win a great victory for African-American rights.

BIRMINGHAM

Martin Luther King Jr. did not limit his activities after the successful boycott in Montgomery. He continued to work to improve the lives of African Americans. In order to accomplish this goal, King founded the Southern Christian Leadership Conference (SCLC) in 1957. King was elected president of the organization. The SCLC headquarters were located in Atlanta. In 1960, King moved to Atlanta to be near the headquarters. He also began to serve as co-pastor with his father at Ebenezer.

One man associated with the SCLC had been fighting segregation for years in Birmingham, Alabama. This man was the Reverend Fred Shuttlesworth. He had suffered many attacks for opposing segregation. In 1956, his house had been bombed on Christmas. He had also been beaten and jailed for his activities. Shuttlesworth urged King to challenge segregation in Birmingham.

In 1963, King decided to accept Shuttlesworth's request. Birmingham was widely considered one of the most segregated cities in the South. King and civil rights activists also wanted to challenge Eugene "Bull" Connor. Birmingham's police and fire departments were run by Connor, who strongly supported segregation. Shuttlesworth believed Connor would react violently to protests. A vicious display of force would reveal to the nation the true nature of Southern racism.

Fred Shuttlesworth talks to activists about segregation.

In Birmingham, King had two goals. First, he wanted to integrate the restaurants in Birmingham's department stores. Second, he wanted to provoke the federal government to become involved with desegregation. King believed that federal laws were needed to abolish segregation of public facilities.

King prepared for demonstrations in Birmingham even though he and Coretta had recently had their fourth child. Bernice was born on March 28, 1963. She joined sister Yolanda, and brothers Martin III and Dexter.

Protests in Birmingham began on April 3. At first, the effort to confront segregation in that city looked as though it might fail. Connor's police officers did not mistreat the protesters. Also, many African Americans declined to join the marches. Soon, a state judge ordered a stop to the marches.

King decided to violate the judge's order. He hoped his defiance would revive the movement. On April 12, King led a march a short way before police arrested him. They put him in Birmingham's jail where he was not allowed to see anyone. But King's arrest had roused the interest of the federal government. U.S. president John F. Kennedy called Coretta King. The president assured her that King would not be harmed.

While in jail, King was able to read newspapers. The *Birmingham News* included a statement from eight white pastors who criticized King's methods. King wrote a response that became known as the "Letter from a Birmingham Jail."

In the letter, King defended the use of nonviolence to achieve justice. He wrote that marches and sit-ins produce a crisis or tension. But this tension leads to negotiation and "will help men rise from the

Three protesters in Birmingham link hands against a powerful stream of water.

dark depths of prejudice and racism to the majestic heights of understanding and brotherhood." King's letter did not receive much attention at first. However, today some consider the letter King's greatest piece of writing.

On April 20, King paid his bail and was freed. He faced a critical situation. The number of marchers continued to fall. Also, the news media had steadily lost interest in the demonstrations. The purpose of the marches was to call attention to the wrongness of segregation. But with the media becoming unconcerned, there was the danger that no one would pay attention to the marches. The movement seemed to be failing.

King's aide, James Bevel, suggested a plan to arouse interest in the marches. He suggested including children in the demonstrations. King and African-American leaders in Birmingham felt uneasy about Bevel's idea. They were concerned that the police might hurt the children. Finally, King agreed that students could be informed about a meeting at the Sixteenth Street Baptist Church.

On May 2, about 1,000 students gathered at the church and began marching toward city hall. The sight of the marching children angered Connor. Police officers arrested several hundred young protesters. School buses were needed to haul away the marchers.

The next day, even more students showed up to march. This time, Connor resorted to cruel methods to control the protesters. Police officers set German shepherds upon the marchers and firefighters blasted the demonstrators with high-pressure hoses. Connor had also brought in a powerful water cannon that swept away marchers.

The news media covered the entire protest. Every day, Americans saw images of the protests on television news broadcasts. Photographs of the violence appeared in newspapers across the nation. Connor's tactics outraged the public. President Kennedy was also upset. He told visitors at the White House that photographs of the violence had sickened him.

The president arranged for a federal official to negotiate a settlement. Birmingham's white business owners agreed to desegregate restaurants at department stores and to hire African-American sales clerks. King was happy with this victory and quickly ended the Birmingham protests. He feared the demonstrators might turn to violence.

TURMOIL

The Sixteenth Street Baptist Church

Martin Luther King Jr.'s work helped the civil rights cause. But outside the marches and the protests, angry whites took out their anger on many African Americans. Birmingham, Alabama, was even called "Bombingham" by some because of racist violence.

On September 15, 1963, at 10:22 AM, four young girls were killed when members of the Ku Klux Klan bombed the Sixteenth Street Baptist Church. Denise McNair, Cynthia Wesley, Addie Mae Collins, and Carole Robertson had been preparing for an 11:00 AM service when the bomb went off. The youngest girl, Denise, was 11 years old. The others were 14.

Rioting followed, and two other teenagers were killed later that day. One was shot in the back by a police officer. The other, 13-year-old Virgil Ware, was shot in the face while bicycling home with his brother.

I HAVE A
DREAM

King now wanted to push for civil rights legislation that would benefit African Americans. In order to do this, King and other African-American leaders planned a march in Washington DC. Some wanted the march to focus on the need for jobs for African Americans. Others wanted it to concentrate on civil rights.

President Kennedy also saw the need for civil rights legislation. On June 11, 1963, he announced his proposal for a civil rights bill in a televised address. Eight days later, the bill was sent to Congress. The bill was momentous. It called for ending segregation in public places such as hotels, restaurants, and theaters. In addition, the bill aimed to increase the federal government's ability to fight segregation.

Congress needed to pass the bill before the legislation could become a law. Kennedy wanted King to cancel the march in Washington DC. The president was worried that a march might offend members of Congress. King and other civil rights leaders disagreed. They believed a march would maintain the pressure to pass a civil rights bill. Later, the march's organizers promised not to cause deliberate disruptions in the city. After that, President Kennedy announced his support for the march.

On August 28, 1963, more than 200,000 people assembled in the capital for the March on Washington for Jobs and Freedom.

King delivers his "I have a dream" speech.

The crowd in front of the Lincoln Memorial offered a portrait of the country's diversity. African Americans, whites, and Hispanics gathered to hear speeches in favor of the president's bill. Millions of other Americans watched the event on television.

King had prepared a speech for the march. But as he spoke, he decided to deliver another speech that he had given on other occasions. This time, however, King had the nation for an audience. In the speech, he described his vision of a society free of prejudice. "I have a dream that one day this nation will rise up and live out the true meaning of its creed: 'We hold these truths to be self-evident— that all men are created equal.'"

The address became known as the "I have a dream" speech. People immediately recognized the power of the speech. Today, it is seen as one of the greatest speeches in U.S. history.

The March on Washington for Jobs and Freedom, however, did not mean success for civil rights legislation. Some members of Congress continued to oppose a civil rights bill. The bill appeared to suffer another setback when Kennedy was assassinated on November 22, 1963, in Dallas, Texas. Vice President Lyndon B. Johnson was quickly sworn in as president. He was a Southerner who had a record of opposing civil rights legislation.

Johnson, however, surprised many people by supporting the civil rights bill. In fact, he strengthened the bill. With Johnson's support, Congress passed the bill. On July 2, 1964, Johnson signed the bill into law. King was among those who attended the signing.

The law signed by Johnson became known as the Civil Rights Act of 1964. It was the most significant piece of civil rights legislation since Reconstruction. The act outlawed segregation in public places. Moreover, the act gave the federal government more power to fight segregation in public schools. Also, employers were prohibited from discriminating on the basis of race, color, sex, or ethnic origin. The act created the Equal Employment Opportunity Commission. This agency

King receives the Nobel Peace Prize from Gunnar Jahn,
chairman of the Norwegian Nobel Peace Prize Committee.

enforces laws that forbid discrimination in matters of employment.

The passage of the Civil Rights Act was not the only triumph that year for King. In October 1964, King learned that he had won the Nobel Peace Prize. The Nobel Committee recognized King for his nonviolent struggle to improve the lives of African Americans. King was 35 years old. At the time, he was the youngest person to have won the Nobel Peace Prize.

American Moments

SELMA

The civil rights movement had made important gains in the 1960s. But there remained a significant problem. In the South, voter discrimination still existed against African Americans. The federal government had attempted to end this discrimination. But Southern states continued to find ways to keep African Americans from registering to vote.

The SCLC targeted Selma, Alabama, as the city to hold marches for voting rights. Selma was an example of voter discrimination in the South. African Americans made up more than half the city's population. However, few African Americans were registered to vote. One incident shows the obstacles that African Americans faced. In 1965, Sheriff Jim Clark struck an African-American woman who tried to register to vote.

Meanwhile, King planned demonstrations around the courthouse in Selma and in nearby counties. During one march in Perry County, law enforcement officers attacked demonstrators with clubs. A young African-American man named Jimmie Lee Jackson was shot and later died. King, who was sick at the time, had not attended the march, but he spoke at Jackson's funeral.

After the funeral, James Bevel wanted to walk to Montgomery to confront Alabama governor George C. Wallace. As governor, Wallace strongly supported segregation and had opposed attempts to integrate

Governor George C. Wallace promises that there will be segregation forever in the state of Alabama.

Alabama's schools. Bevel's remark led to an idea for a march from Selma to Montgomery. Wallace vowed to block the march. Bevel encouraged King to stay out of the march because of concerns about safety.

On March 7, 1965, more than 500 demonstrators gathered at Brown Chapel in Selma. They intended to march 54 miles (87 km) to Montgomery. At the Edmund Pettus Bridge, the marchers encountered law enforcement officers on horseback and state troopers. The marchers stopped but did not turn around. Next, the troopers advanced and attacked the demonstrators with clubs. Then, they

An Alabama state trooper stands next to an unconscious protester in Selma, Alabama, after police have broken up the march to Montgomery.

fired tear gas. Mounted officers drove the marchers toward Brown Chapel. In total, about 70 demonstrators suffered injuries in the attack.

Television cameras and newspaper photographers recorded images of the violence. The brutality had the same effect as the cruel tactics used in Birmingham. Across the country, people were furious. Thousands protested in the United States and Canada in support of the Selma marchers. President Johnson appeared before Congress to insist on the passage of a voting rights bill.

King and his aides soon planned another march from Selma to Montgomery. This march promised to have a different result. Wallace said Alabama could not afford the costs of protecting the marchers. However, Johnson provided federal officials and military police to guard the marchers. He also put more than 1,800 Alabama National Guardsmen into federal service to protect the demonstrators.

On March 21, more than 3,000 marchers arrived at Brown Chapel. This time, King led the march along Highway 80 toward Montgomery. As they proceeded toward the state capital, thousands of other people joined the demonstrators. But many angry whites also lined the roads to taunt the protestors. By March 25, the demonstration had reached Montgomery, and the number of participants had grown to about 25,000.

In Montgomery, the marchers gathered at the capitol building. They had brought a petition that supported voting rights and condemned police brutality. The demonstrators wished to present the petition to Wallace, but he remained inside the capitol.

Governor Wallace avoided the marchers, but they won the fight for voting rights. On August 4, 1965, Congress passed the Voting Rights Act. Two days later, Johnson signed it into law. The act suspended literacy tests and other methods designed to keep African Americans from registering to vote. Also, the act allowed federal examiners to supervise voter registration and to observe polling places.

The Voting Rights Act of 1965 made a major difference in the lives of African Americans. Within a year, another 300,000 African Americans had registered to vote. Throughout the South, the percentage of registered African-American voters climbed. In 1964, only 19 percent of the African Americans eligible to vote in Alabama were registered. By 1969, that number had jumped to 69 percent. Eventually, Southern politicians such as George Wallace had to consider the needs of African-American voters. In addition, many African Americans ran for office and were elected in the South.

King and his supporters marched in Selma, Alabama, in 1965 for voting rights because they knew that getting access to the vote would create change. "Do you realize what would happen," King said, "if three million Negro voters were added to the rolls in the South?"

In 1964, half a million African Americans were not registered to vote in Alabama alone. Throughout the South, about four million eligible African Americans were not registered to vote. That many voters could change the whole political makeup of the South.

Also, African Americans would finally be able to use their vote to stop some of the injustices that they suffered. Poverty, segregation, and discrimination were all major concerns. King knew that many of these issues could be improved once whites stopped blocking African Americans from voting.

THE MOUNTAINTOP

During the next two years, King widened the scope of his concerns. He wanted to address the problem of poverty among all races in the United States. In order to do this, King established the Poor People's Campaign. As part of the campaign, King planned to bring thousands of demonstrators to Washington DC. There, they would live in tents and demand that the federal government do more to fight poverty. If the government refused, the demonstrators would disrupt the capital.

Meanwhile, James Lawson invited King to come to Memphis to support striking sanitation workers. Lawson was King's friend and a pastor at a Methodist church in Memphis. King agreed to help. The workers were the kind of people the Poor People's Campaign was trying to assist. King arrived in Memphis to give speeches and to talk with Lawson. A demonstration was scheduled for March 28, 1968.

The march took place that day, but it failed to conform to King's belief in nonviolence. Young, militant African-American men began smashing store windows. Police responded by beating demonstrators and using tear gas. One African-American teenager was shot and killed by police. King left the march in a car that was driving by the scene. He was deeply troubled by the violence.

King remained committed to helping the workers. On April 3, he delivered a speech at Mason Temple church in Memphis. King told

A Memphis police officer stands guard over a suspected store looter on March 28, 1968.

the audience that the struggle for racial equality was challenging. But he believed that racial harmony would be achieved in the future. "We've got some difficult days ahead. But it doesn't matter with me now, because I've been to the mountaintop."

King also planned to hold another march for the sanitation workers. He hoped this demonstration would be better organized and avoid violence. The march was scheduled for April 8 to give King and other leaders more time to prepare for a peaceful demonstration.

King never led the march. On April 4, he was struck by a .30-06 bullet while standing on the balcony of the Lorraine Motel. The murder prompted a search for the killer. The Federal Bureau of Investigation (FBI) suspected James Earl Ray of shooting King. Ray had a criminal history and resented African Americans. While in prison, he opposed being sent to an integrated prison. In 1967, Ray escaped from prison in Missouri.

The assassination set off violence throughout the United States. Riots broke out in more than 100 cities as African Americans expressed their anger over King's death. Thousands of U.S. soldiers and National Guard members were called in to secure the cities. Even so, at least 39 people died in the riots and thousands were injured. Some of the worst violence occurred in Washington DC. But by April 11, most of the rioting had died down.

Almost two months later, authorities arrested Ray at Heathrow Airport near London, England. Ray was taken to Memphis where he pleaded guilty to King's murder on March 10, 1969. He received a 99-year prison sentence. Later, Ray claimed he was not guilty of the assassination. Instead, Ray insisted that a conspiracy was responsible for King's death.

Dexter King visits the grave of his father, Martin Luther King Jr.

Some have come to believe that others beside Ray were involved in King's death. King's family had requested another trial for Ray in order to discover more information about the assassination. However, Ray died in prison in 1998 before a trial was ever held.

Although King's life ended when he was only 39 years old, he had accomplished amazing triumphs for civil rights. But King's struggle for a better society did not end with his death. The King Center in Atlanta continues his work. The organization is dedicated to building a more peaceful and just world. While the United States has not reached the mountaintop of King's vision, the nation has begun the climb toward greater racial equality. Thanks to King's courage, the country has progressed a long way from the segregated buses in Montgomery.

TIMELINE

1929 Martin Luther King Jr. is born on January 15.

1953 In June, King marries Coretta Scott.

1954 King becomes the pastor at Dexter Avenue Baptist Church in Montgomery, Alabama.

1955 to 1956 Rosa Parks refuses to give up her seat on a segregated bus, sparking the Montgomery Bus Boycott. King is elected president of the Montgomery Improvement Association (MIA), which manages the boycott. The boycott ends after the U.S. Supreme Court declares segregation on the city's buses illegal.

1957 King founds the Southern Christian Leadership Conference (SCLC).

1963 In April and May, King and his supporters stage marches and protests in Birmingham, Alabama, against segregation. King also writes his "Letter from a Birmingham Jail."

On August 28, more than 200,000 people gather in Washington DC for the March on Washington for Jobs and Freedom. King gives his famous "I have a dream" speech.

1964 On July 2, President Lyndon B. Johnson signs the Civil Rights Act of 1964 into law.

In October, King wins the Nobel Peace Prize.

1965 In March, King and his supporters organize marches for voting rights from Selma to Montgomery in Alabama.

On August 4, Congress passes the Voting Rights Act of 1965.

1968 On March 28, King leads a march in Memphis, Tennessee, for sanitation workers' rights. The march ends abruptly after turning violent.

On April 3, King gives his "I've been to the mountaintop" speech.

On April 4, King is assassinated by James Earl Ray at the Lorraine Motel in Memphis.

American Moments

FAST FACTS

Martin Luther King Jr. had several threats to his life after the Montgomery Bus Boycott. A second bomb was found on his front porch on January 27, 1957. King was also stabbed in Harlem, New York, the following year by a mentally ill woman. In August 1966, angry whites in Chicago, Illinois, stoned King.

King received numerous awards and honors for his work toward racial equality. Besides winning the Nobel Peace Prize, King made the cover of *Time* magazine in 1957. He became *Time*'s "Man of the Year" in 1963. King also earned more than 20 honorary degrees from various universities. He won the Marcus Garvey Award for Human Rights in 1968.

During his lifetime, King wrote six books. They were *Stride Toward Freedom: The Montgomery Story*, *The Measure of a Man*, *Why We Can't Wait*, *Strength to Love*, *Where Do We Go From Here: Chaos or Community?*, and *The Trumpet of Conscience*.

On November 3, 1983, President Ronald Regan signed legislation that made the third Monday of January a national holiday honoring Martin Luther King Jr. The first holiday was observed in 1986.

In 1999, the case of *Coretta Scott King, Martin Luther King III, Bernice King, Dexter Scott King, and Yolanda King v. Loyd Jowers and Other Unknown Conspirators* was decided. In this civil trial, a jury found Loyd Jowers, the City of Memphis, the state of Tennessee, and the federal government guilty of conspiring to murder Martin Luther King Jr. The federal government, however, has not found conclusive evidence pointing to a conspiracy.

WEB SITES
WWW.ABDOPUB.COM

Would you like to learn more about the Assassination of Martin Luther King Jr.? Please visit **www.abdopub.com** to find up-to-date Web site links about the assassination of Martin Luther King Jr. and other American moments. These links are routinely monitored and updated to provide the most current information available.

King speaks to a crowd in Selma, Alabama,
that is about to march to Montgomery.

American Moments

GLOSSARY

amendment: a change to a country's constitution.

assassinate: to murder a very important person.

bail: money given to authorities in exchange for releasing someone from jail. It is also a guarantee that the released person will appear at his or her trial.

civil rights: the individual rights of a citizen, such as the right to vote or freedom of speech.

conspiracy: a joining together of two or more people to commit a crime. Conspiracy is also used to describe an evil act that seems to have been planned.

discrimination: treating a group of people unfairly based on characteristics such as race, class, or gender.

inherent: a natural quality in a person, thing, or situation.

lawsuit: a case brought to court because of a perceived wrong.

leaflets: pieces of paper with words or pictures giving people information.

literacy: the ability to read and write.

minstrel: a lyric poet, musician, or singer of folk songs. In the United States, minstrels were white performers who blackened their faces and pretended to be slaves in the mid-1800s. Their impersonations were usually very prejudiced.

negotiate: to discuss an issue in order to reach an agreement.

ordained: given the authority to be a priest or minister.

precedent: a ruling in an earlier court case that can be applied to later court cases.

racism: a belief that one race is better than another.

Reconstruction: the period of time after the Civil War when laws were passed to help the Southern states rebuild and return to the Union.

sanitation: the act of making clean. Sanitation workers collect garbage and do other tasks that maintain public health.

seminary: a school that trains people to become priests or ministers.

sociology: the study of society.

theology: the study of religion and of God.

unconstitutional: not consistent with the Constitution.

INDEX